1995

To the trees of the forest

Look to see how the trees are pollinated.

wind

insects

Text copyright © 1990 by Judy Hindley
Illustrations copyright © 1990 by Alison Wisenfeld
All rights reserved. No part of this book may be reproduced or transmitted in any form or by any
means, electronic or mechanical, including photocopying, recording, or by any information
storage and retrieval system, without permission in writing from the publisher.
Published in the United States by Clarkson N. Potter, Inc., a Random House company,
distributed by Crown Publishers, Inc., 201 East 50th Street, New York, New York 10022.
First published 1990 in Great Britain by Aurum Books for Children, London

CLARKSON N. POTTER, POTTER, and colophon are trademarks of Clarkson N. Potter, Inc.

Printed and bound in Italy by LEGO

Library of Congress Cataloging-in-Publication Data

Hindley, Judy.
    The tree.

    Summary: Lyrical text and poetic words provide information about trees.
    1. Trees — Juvenile literature.   [1. Trees]
QK475.8.H56 1990   582.16   89-16105
                ISBN 0-517-57630-9

      10   9   8   7   6   5   4   3   2   1

                First American edition

THE TREE

Written by
Judy Hindley

Illustrated by
Alison Wisenfeld

Clarkson N. Potter, Inc./Publishers
201 EAST 50TH STREET
NEW YORK, NEW YORK 10022

Hawthorn

The May Tree

as oak and ash
and hawthorn tree
live, leaf and witness me
believe what I promise thee

(Crataegus)

The hawthorn is named for its berries (haws) and for its long, spiny thorns, which are really branches that never grow. This tree makes a strong, fierce hedge, good for keeping animals safe on their grazing land, away from farmers' crops.

In the spring, this stiff, little, curly-leaved tree foams with blossom — white or pink or red — as soft as cream. Long ago, when our calendar was different, the hawthorn bloomed for May Day, so its second name is the May Tree. It was a favorite flower for May-poles, spring festivals and wedding processions.

In ancient times, the hawthorn was thought to be a fairy tree, particularly if it stood alone. It was also one of the three trees that people called upon to make a special promise. They would say, "By oak, ash and thorn", meaning that their word was as true and real as these three trees.

Ash

The Lucky Tree

curving twiglets
tipped with soot
bundles of keys
lucky leaves
limbs that fork
like a catapult

(Fraxinus)

In winter, look for forking branches, up-curved twigs jewelled with soot-black leaf-buds, and hanging bundles of dried seed-keys. In spring the ash sprouts leaves in bunches, like tufts of yellow-green feathers. Its leafing time is thought to predict rain: "Oak before ash, only a splash; Ash before oak, soak, soak, soak."

This friendly, useful tree burns more easily than other wood. Its close-grained timber is tough and flexible and smooth — handy for anything that is gripped from the spears of ancient times to hockey sticks, as well as shovels, rakes and all the furniture of a farmyard.

Look out for a leaf with an even number of leaflets — few things are luckier than an even-leaved ash.

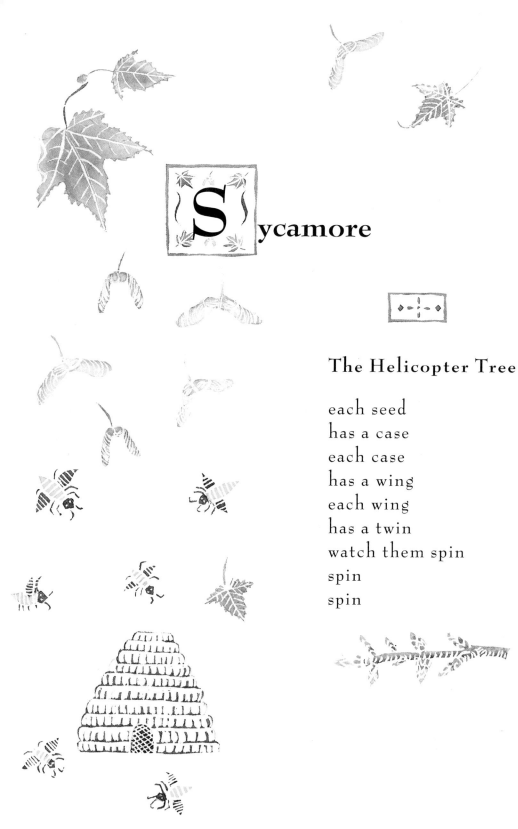

Sycamore

The Helicopter Tree

each seed
has a case
each case
has a wing
each wing
has a twin
watch them spin
spin
spin

(Acer)

One of the best things about a sycamore tree is its spinners. These are the seed-cases, which look like pairs of drooping wings. All through the last months of summer, you can see the sycamore sending off these tiny helicopters ... toss them into the air and watch them twirl!

A sycamore grows very tall and spreading, so its seeds need to get away to find enough space to grow. This isn't true of its little cousin, the field maple, which grows its seed-cases in a nearly straight line.

The North American sugar maple is a particularly spectacular relative. Its raggedy leaves turn scarlet and yellow in the autumn. Its sap is so sweet that people run it off into buckets in early spring, and boil it up into syrup and fragrant brown sugar.

Horse-Chestnut

The Conker Tree

conkers
in the autumn
candles
in the spring

(Aesculus)

In the spring, when the tree is bare, it is studded with big, golden buds, all pointing up, that seem to be covered with a sticky varnish. The buds are leaf-cases. Inside each is a tiny fan of baby leaves and, sometimes, the spike of a miniature flower. (If you put a budding branch in water, you can watch it open day by day.) As the leaves unfurl, the bud breaks open and out pops a limp umbrella of frilly leaves. Then, the leaves spread out like big hands, and the flower spike fattens and stretches and bursts into bloom, until the tree is covered with huge, fat candles of pink or white flowers.

In the autumn, when the flowers have withered, their spiky green fruits split open and scatter seeds – bigger than marbles, dark and smooth. For hundreds of years children have threaded these on strings to knock against one another, testing which cracks and which is stronger. This game is called "conkers", because of the sound the seeds make when they collide.

Willow

The best place to find willows is in a valley, along the line of a river-bed. Willows love to be near water. Look for a misty thicket of skinny branches, or a quivering screen of narrow, spear-shaped leaves.

The twig of a crack-willow snaps right off if it is tapped at the base. Its bark peels like an orange, leaving a smooth, white stem, like a bendy bone. That's what "wicker" is — young, supple willow shoots that can be woven into chairs and baskets and even boats, like the round little hide-covered coracles used since Bible times.

The pretty weeping willow, with its trailing branches, is one of the first trees to leaf in spring time.

But one of the best things of all is the catkins, flowers of the willow. Take home a budding branch in early spring and watch them ripen — small and silver, like buds of fur, or long and golden as a kitten's tail.

(Salix)

The Catkin Tree

switches   whistles   rods and baskets

cradles   coracles   and furry catkins

Fir

These trees have needles instead of leaves. Pines have bundles of long needles that grow in pairs; firs are like bottle-brushes with little needles all over.

Both are called CONifers — because they have cones. A fir has a little ruffley cone, like a flower made of bark. A pine-cone grows bigger. It starts closed and knobbly, but as it ripens its wooden "petals" uncurl, scattering its seeds, which have very sweet white kernels.

The soft wood of firs grows fast, so they are harvested quickly to make paper. You can imagine them as a forest of books and newspapers! Pines are often used to make tables and dressers.

A forest of conifers is hushed and secret. The trees grow close together, straight as soldiers, so that all paths look alike.

These were the great, dark forests of the fairytales in days when bears and wolves roamed. Yet, even then, green conifer boughs in winter were a sign of hope, reminding people of the spring — and that's how the fir tree came to be our Christmas tree.

(Abies)

(Pinus)

The Hush-a-Bye Tree

golden needles
soft as moss
wind in the boughs
roars softly,
"hush…"

no leaf
no flower
where it stands,
smells like Christmas
on your hands

Beech

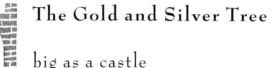

The Gold and Silver Tree

big as a castle

cool as a cave

calm as a church

green as a wave

(fagus)

Its trunk is smooth and silver. Its small, crisp leaves turn golden in autumn. It is a kingly tree, so strong and calm, often planted as a hedge to shield more fragile trees.

It makes a cave of green in the summer, like a hollow of a wave. Flowers often nestle within its twisted roots in spring. The beech-mast — nut-like fruits that fall in autumn — keeps away scrubby undergrowth.

Listen to the sound the wind makes in its leaves. Each kind of tree has its own sound — whispering, rustling, roaring, moaning. Some people know trees by their sounds. A big, old beech has a high, soft hiss like a wave as its foam curls round a rock. Listen...

Birch

The Paper-Bark Tree

who was there
when mammoths roamed?
who was there
when the woods were free?
who stands brave
in a waste of cold?
slender, dancing
paper-bark tree

(Betula)

This is a much-beloved tree. Once you've seen one, you will always recognize it, even in the winter. It has a straight, long trunk, slim as a pencil — white or cream or, sometimes, palest pink — marked with rows of tiny stitches and dark diamond shapes. Its bark peels away like a curl of paper with a silky lining. In summer, the birch has a veil of tiny, triangular leaves, that lightly dance and tremble.

This delicate looking tree has only a human life-span. Yet it belongs to an ancient tree-family, whose bark made fishing-floats for Stone Age people, as well as wigwams and canoes for many of the first people in North America.

The birch is so strong that it survives even beyond the Arctic Circle and in the snowy wastes of Siberia — a sign of cheerfulness and hope for the people there, who are so grateful to see their dancing trees again, at the end of the seven-month snows.

P lane

The Itchy-Ball Tree

dingly,
dangly,
itchy-ball tree
for green
for shade
in parks
and streets

spots
and blotches
going up,
leaves
in heaps
beneath
your feet

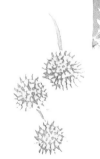

(Platanus)

A plane tree grows new bark like a change of clothes — always peeling, patching and "dressing" itself. Its glossy leaves are easily washed by rain. These things protect it from the dirty city air — that's why you see it on so many city streets.

The plane has a seed-ball like a thistle, with the downy seeds pressed together in the center, and the tails sticking out in a prickly ball. They dangle from the trees all through the winter. Then, as they ripen, they explode! And the itchy seeds go flying.

Look for a slender, elegant tree, with a mottled trunk, like a giraffe. Look for branches held out wide, draped with a flutter of leaves like pointy lace… leaves to scuffle through in autumn. And look for seed-balls hanging delicately from slim, bare twigs in winter.

That's a plane tree.

E lm

The Quiet Tree

the tall elms
that marched against the sky
the tall elms
that arched above the lane
the tall elms
that died so suddenly —
the elms are coming back
to us again

(Ulmus)

The elm is a tree of memory, for many people. It is in old paintings of the countryside, especially around churchyards, making long columns of shadow – a tall, rather weedy tree, like a great high tower of leaves in summer. Its timber was often used in church pews, baby furniture and toys.

People loved the elm. It was like a good old soldier, strong and reliable, always there for shade. The murmur of its leaves was a friendly country sound. It seemed a tree that always had been, and always would be.

Then a terrible illness killed the elms in only a few years. The tall guardians vanished and, with them, the habitat of many creeping, flying creatures. Birds such as rooks who built colonies of nests in the elms' high branches had to find new homes.

But around the big stumps of the old elms, saplings began to shoot up from the roots, which hadn't been hurt by the disease. Now in some places, there are whole hedges of elm.

The elms are coming back.

Apple

The Climbing Tree

for pies
for cider
for crunching
for dunking
for wooden spoons
for violins

for mosses
crochets
honey-bees
for spring
for scent
for climbing in

(Malus.)

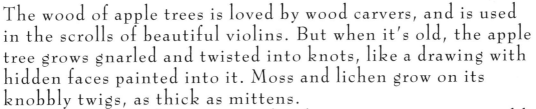

The wood of apple trees is loved by wood carvers, and is used in the scrolls of beautiful violins. But when it's old, the apple tree grows gnarled and twisted into knots, like a drawing with hidden faces painted into it. Moss and lichen grow on its knobbly twigs, as thick as mittens.

If you crush and press an apple, the sugar in its juice quickly turns to bubbles, making cider. Sometimes, wasps get nearly drunk on fallen apples — perhaps the apples bubble into cider in the sun.

If you have an apple tree nearby, you can watch its apples start to grow, from the tiny bulge at the end of a twig, when the blossom falls, to the big, sweet lump that stubs your toes among the leaves and grass in autumn.

There are so many kinds of apples in different shapes and colours — round, long, heart-shaped; shades of gold and yellow and green and white and crimson.

Oak

The Magic Tree

pigs lived on it
deer lived under it
druids sang to it
ships sailed in it
birds nested in it
Robin hid in it

(Quercus)

You will know the oak tree by its acorn and curly leaf, and the rather spooky, ragged shape it has in winter, with its thick, crooked boughs and bristly twigs like crooked little fingers.

In ancient times, the oak was thought to be a magic tree, and druid leaders sang to it.

Robin Hood and his followers lurked in its branches, that spread so broad and safe.

This tree has been a friend to people for a long, long time. Its acorns fed the herds of wild pigs and deer that people lived on, and its timber made houses and furniture and sailing ships.

It was said that anyone who really loved his country would never go anywhere without a handful of acorns to plant, so that the land would never, ever run out of oak trees.